AF574775

THE VICTORIAN SOLDIERS & SAILORS BOOK

COMPILED BY
VIVIEN NOAKES

COLLINS

BUM-BOAT.

This book, and the others in the series, has been compiled from *Things In-Doors* and *Things Out-of-Doors,* children's question and answer books published during the 1860s. They were designed particularly for use in the home, where the child's mother or governess would supervise the learning of facts by heart.

ISBN 0 00 195744 9

Made and printed in Great Britain by
William Collins Sons & Co Ltd Glasgow

PARADE.

Wellington, who led the British to victory over Napoleon in 1815, described the ordinary British soldiers as 'the scum of the earth'. In their scarlet coats they had fought bravely and well, but the conditions in which they lived did not attract good men into the army. Enlistment was for life, punishments were severe, living quarters bad and the food inadequate. Throughout Victoria's reign, however, things improved, hastened by the revelations of the Crimean War in the mid-1850s where, for every soldier killed, seven died of illness or exposure. With better conditions came pride, and the cheerful image of Tommy Atkins.

The Navy also began the century victoriously at the Battle of Trafalgar in 1805, the last great sea battle to be fought by the British under sail. In the peaceful years which followed, the navy underwent change. The introduction of steam in the 1850s at first supplemented sail and later replaced it, whilst the 1860s saw the strengthening of wooden ships with armour plates of iron, until gradually wooden hulls disappeared entirely and the modern navy was born.

PIONEER.

RECRUIT.

What is a recruit?
A man who has recently joined the army.

What is joining the army called?
Enlisting.

What is the first duty of the recruit?
To learn to march in quick or slow time, to handle his rifle, and to load and fire correctly.

What is a soldier?
A fighting man who does battle on land as one of an army.

Do you mean one who is paid by the state?
Yes, his name is probably taken from the Latin word *solidus*.

What does that mean?
A shilling; and a shilling is the coin given to a recruit when he joins the army.

FOOT-SOLDIER.

BARRACK.

What is a barrack?
A large building in which soldiers live.

Where are barracks built?
In towns or cities where regiments are stationed.

How do soldiers live where there are no barracks?
They are quartered at taverns or other places.

What is a garrison?
The troops who guard a fort or a fortified town.

Where are garrisons placed?
Generally near a seaport or dockyard.

Why?
Because such places require protection, and also that the soldiers may readily embark on board ship for foreign service.

GARRISON.

Who is the sergeant?
A non-commissioned officer who instructs recruits in their exercise.

What other duty does he do?
He inspects and trains the soldiers in their duty.

Who acts under the sergeant?
The corporal.

SERGEANT.

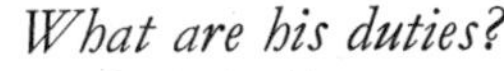

What are his duties?
Very nearly the same as those of the sergeant, from whom he takes his orders.

SENTINEL.

What is a sentinel?
A soldier placed on guard.

What is his duty?
To watch the safety of some place, or to give notice of the approach of danger.

How long does he remain on duty?
Till he is relieved.

CAVALRY.

What is a cavalry regiment?
Eight troops of horse-soldiers, under the command of a lieutenant-colonel.

Which are the Hussars?
Light horse-soldiers, so called because they formerly used to shout in battle.

What is the Hussar uniform?
A fur hat with a coloured bag and tassel coming from the top: and a loose outer jacket hanging from one shoulder. The latter is not now worn.

HUSSAR.

What is a lancer?
A horse-soldier carrying a long lance or spear.

Is he of the light or heavy cavalry?
Of the light cavalry, his duty often being to carry messages and orders on the field.

LANCER.

CUIRASSIER.

Who is a cuirassier?
A horse guard in the French army, so called from his cuirass or armour.

Has the helmet feathers in it?
No; a long streamer made of a horse-tail.

ARTILLERYMAN.

Who is an artilleryman?

One of the soldiers who has charge of the field-pieces.

What are field-pieces?

Guns mounted on light carriages and drawn by horses.

What are this kind of guns called?

Light artillery.

For what is it used?

For firing at the enemy as he advances or retreats.

FIELD-PIECE.

What is an engineer?

One of the soldiers whose duty it is to make trenches, earthworks, &c.

ENGINEER.

What is a trench?

A long ditch or opening cut in the ground, and hidden by a high bank.

What is its use?

To defend an army in the field, the bank screening them from the foe.

What is the first making of the trenches called?

Opening the trenches.

TRENCH.

For what else are trenches used?

They are sometimes cut towards a fortress that is to be attacked.

FORT.

What is a fort?

A strong building to protect the entrance to a town.

Is it always to protect a town?

Sometimes it protects a harbour or sea-coast from the attacks of ships of war.

What is a bastion?

A sort of fort generally placed at the angles of a fortification.

How is it built?

Generally of earth; sometimes with stone or brick.

BASTION.

REDOUBT.

What is a redoubt?
A small fort generally erected on a height, and defended only in the front.

In what great war were these forts used?
In the war in the Crimea, when the English and French conquered the Russian army.

What is a palisade?
A row of pointed stakes in front of a fortification.

What are stakes?
Long pointed poles of wood or iron.

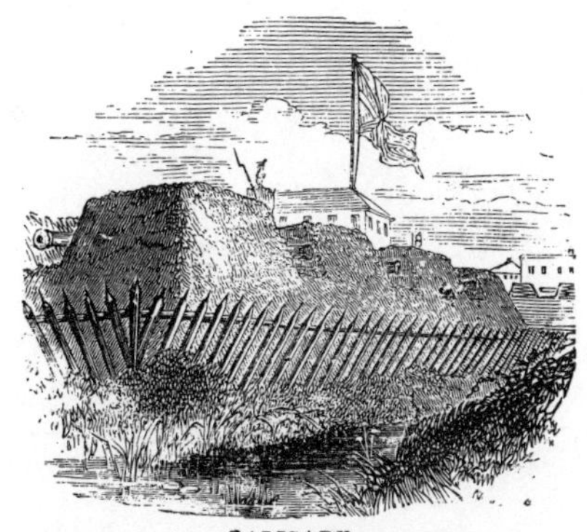

PALISADE.

REVIEW.

SALUTE.

What is a review?
A number of troops assembled to go through the various movements and exercises.

Before whom do they do this?
Generally before some great personage, or the commander-in-chief.

Do they perform all the exercises required in battle?
Not always. When they do so it is called a "sham fight".

What is a salute?
A number of guns fired in honour of some great person or event.

Is there any other way of saluting?
Yes, a private soldier salutes an officer, and officers salute their superior officers.

FLAG.

What is a flag?
A large piece of woven canvas or silk of various colours, or containing some emblematical design.

What is its use?
It is fastened to a pole or staff and hoisted as a signal.

When the flags have national arms or emblems upon them what are they called?
Ensigns.

What is a fleet?
A number of ships together in one place and for one purpose.

Is a fleet composed of vessels of war?
Yes; but a number of trading or merchant ships are sometimes called a fleet.

But not THE *fleet?*
No; when speaking of the fleet or the navy, we always mean the vessels of war.

FLEET.

SHIP-YARD.

What is a ship-yard?
An immense yard at the waterside, where ships and boats are built.

Where are the principal ship-yards in Great Britain?
Along the Thames, near London; the Mersey, near Birkenhead; the Severn at Bristol; and on the Clyde and the Humber.

Who is the boat-builder?
The person who forms and builds small sailing vessels and rowing boats.

BOAT-BUILDER.

What is the business of the shipwright?
The constructing and fitting together of the frame of the ship.

SHIPWRIGHT.

Of what are ships built?
Many are now built of iron, but trading vessels are generally of wood.

KEEL.

What is the keel?
The lowest and principal timber at the bottom of the ship.

What is its use?
It supports the whole frame of the hull.

How is the keel made?
Of several pieces of timber bolted together; sometimes of iron.

BOAT.

What is a boat?
A small vessel, generally without a sail.

How is it moved?
By rowing.

What is rowing?
Moving a boat in the water by means of long pieces of wood with flat blades at their ends.

What are these called?
The larger are called oars, the smaller sculls.

What is a jolly-boat?
A small sea boat carried at the stern of a ship.

Are ships compelled to carry small boats with them on a voyage?
Yes; large vessels, even in the merchant service, carry seven boats.

What are those boats called?
In merchant vessels they are called launches, pinnaces, cutters, or dingys.

JOLLY-BOAT.

CRAFT.

What is a craft?
It is another name for a small sailing vessel.

Are boats without sails called craft?
Not usually—small craft have generally one mast, and two or more sails.

Name some of the smaller kinds of vessels called craft.
Yachts, sloops, yawls, cutters, luggers, and smacks.

What is a cutter?
A small one-masted vessel carrying only fore and aft sails.

Is there not also a boat called a cutter?
Yes; one of the boats belonging to a ship.

What is it used for?
For conveying the officers ashore.

For any other purpose?
In time of war for rowing to a ship which is to be taken.

CUTTER.

BRIG.

What is a brig?
A two-masted sailing vessel.

What sails does a brig carry?
A full-rigged brig carries square sails at both masts.

What is a schooner?
A two-masted vessel not carrying all square sails on either mast.

What is a fore and aft schooner?
One that has only fore and aft sails and no topsails.

What is the mast nearest the head of a ship called?
The fore-mast.

SCHOONER.

What is a barque?
A three-masted ship with square sails on only two of her masts.

Which two masts have square sails?
The fore-mast and the main-mast.

What is the other mast?
The mizen-mast, which is nearest the stern.

BARQUE.

SHIP.

What is a ship?
A three-masted vessel.

Does it differ from a barque?
Yes; it has square sails on all three masts.

In any other way?
No; except that barques are smaller vessels, and are only used as merchant ships.

FRIGATE.

What is a frigate?
A ship of war having only one tier or row of guns.

What do you mean by an iron-clad steamer?
A war steamer, the hull of which is coated with plates of iron.

How are these plates made?
They are beaten and wrought with a steam hammer.

WAR STEAMER.

Are all ships moved by means of sails alone?
No; a great number are now moved by steam.

STEAM-VESSEL.

How is this done?
By a steam-engine in the lower part of the vessel.

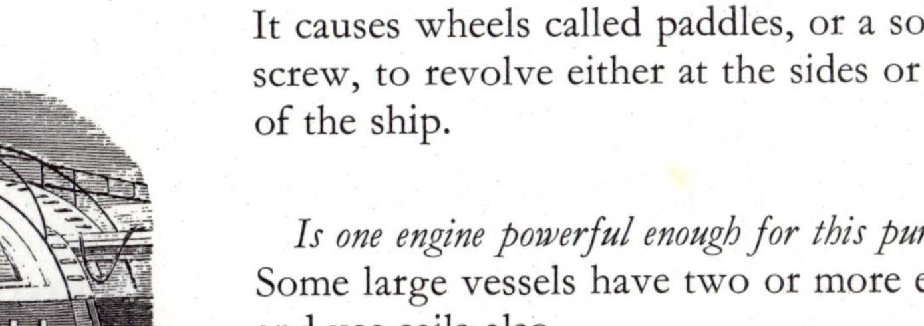

What does this engine do?
It causes wheels called paddles, or a sort of bladed screw, to revolve either at the sides or the stern of the ship.

PADDLE-BOX.

Is one engine powerful enough for this purpose?
Some large vessels have two or more engines, and use sails also.

What kind of vessels are moved by steam?
Those carrying passengers, and which go at great speed.

ANCHOR.

What is an anchor?
A great iron implement, with a forked and pointed end.

What is its use?
It is fastened to a cable, and sunk to the bottom of the water, to hold ships fast.

Why is it forked?
That it may enter the ground and have a firm hold.

What is a capstan?
A machine placed on the deck of the ship for the purpose of raising the anchor.

CAPSTAN.

SHOT.

What are shot?

Great bullets of iron fired from ships' cannon.

What is a round shot?

A large bullet of iron.

What is case shot?

A number of smaller bullets in a case which bursts on being fired.

What are shells?

Hollow bullets filled with a composition which explodes after they are fired.

What are bar-shot?

Two bullets joined by a bar and fired to cut away masts and rigging.

What is the duty of the gunner?

To point and fire the gun when a ship is engaged in battle.

What else has he to do?

To see that the guns are in good order, and ready for use, and to see to the supply of shot.

GUNNER.

BOATSWAIN.

Who is the boatswain?
An inferior officer in the navy.

What is his duty?
He has charge of the rigging of the ship.

What is the rigging?
The ropes, shrouds, and ratlines.

What else does the boatswain do?
He calls the men to their duty by sounding his whistle.

Who are boatmen?
Men who row passengers on rivers or take them to ships lying off a shore.

BOATMAN.

HELMSMAN.

Who is the helmsman?
The man who steers a ship or boat.

Is the ship steered by one man?
Sometimes by two men, in rough weather; in large ships of war several men are required.

What is the duty of the helmsman?
To keep the course, or to alter it, according to the orders of the officer on duty.

Who is the cockswain?
The man who steers a rowing boat.

COCKSWAIN.

What is a beacon?
A fire lit on the top of a hill or watch-tower, for a signal.

When is it lit?
It is not often used now, but it was formerly used in time of war.

BEACON.

LIGHT-HOUSE.

What is the use of a light-house?
It warns sailors that they are near a dangerous coast.

Why is it called a light-house?
Because a very bright light is burnt in it.

Are the lights all the same?
No; some burn steadily, some flash, and some are only seen at intervals.

STORM.

What is a storm at sea?
Violent wind, sometimes with heavy rain and lightning.

What are these violent winds sometimes called?
Hurricanes.

What is their effect?
To agitate the waves of the sea, and increase their force against the ship.

What is a life-boat?
A boat so built that it will float or even go through the waves in a heavy sea.

LIFE-BOAT.

ROCK.

What is a rock?
A large piece of stone standing out of the earth.

When rocks are near the sea to what do they change?
The water washes against them, and crumbles them into small pieces.

What is a shore formed of these pieces called?
Shingle.

When the waves dash against a rock, what do they form?
Breakers.

SHINGLE.

CLIFF.

What is a cliff?
A high part of the sea-shore, mostly formed of layers or beds of rock.

What are often found in cliffs?
The nests and eggs of sea-gulls and other sea birds.

Name one of the most celebrated cliffs in England.
Shakespeare's cliff, near Dover.

What is a harbour?
A place of safety for ships that have made their voyage, or are compelled to wait for fair weather.

HARBOUR.

HULK.